There weren't a hoss that couldn't be rode.
And never a cowboy that couldn't be throwed!

~ Some Cowboy
   Back In Some Day

Design by BookCreate
Seattle, Washington USA

Printed in USA

ISBN 978-1-54397-479-9

JUST FOR THE HELLUVIT

David Ullman

A Personal Note

There's no telling just where or when a cowboy said "I don't think you can ride that there bronc!" To which the second cowboy replied "Could be, but I wouldn't bet a dollar on it!" It was probably like that... the first cowboy competition.

It's a lot different today. TV, big sponsors, big bucks. Pro Rodeo.

Happily the original cowboy spirit is still found in local "Ranch Rodeos" in Alberta, Saskatchewan, British Columbia, and most of the Western United States. Today working cowboys compete as amateurs the way they did back when "...bet a dollar ...!" was all the challenge needed. The prize money may be small but the winner's buckles are big and bragging rights never tarnish.

Granted, cowboy competitions have changed somewhat. Events like penning, wild cow milking and team roping are fun. But, when a chute opens and a saddle bronc charges out into the arena heart rates increase! In my view, Saddle Bronc riding is the classic cowboy event.

An old horseman once told me you could tell everything you needed to know about a horse by looking into its eyes. Over the years I've looked into a lot of horse eyes. And I'll tell you this: for the most part they just looked back at me. That's about it. But every now and then I saw a glimpse of something that said "be careful; I'm special!" These are special horses. They're athletes. They come from all over. And while some are bred to buck some just don't like being ridden. That noted, they all love to buck off riders. Just for the helluvit.

deu

Virginia

The colt was cantankerous from Day 1. But he was built perfectly; powerful hindquarters and a broad chest. Overall, a look of strength and power. If someone could handle him he'd make a real Timber Racer.

At the same time…

… in Alberta

The mare was bigger than most. Major attitude. A swift kick to a lusty colt straightened him out. When she played, you could see her athleticism. The way she leaped and twisted and kicked up her heels. She'd be tough to train, but she'd make a fine show jumper.

Meanwhile…

… in South Dakota

You could see the Thoroughbred in him. Long legs, big chest and a strong, powerful butt. Faster than lightning, too. A natural runner with the right rider. If the right rider could stay on. Perfect for the upcoming series of tribal races.

Right then…

... in California

Good breeding shows. The colt was handsome, A bright Chestnut with four white feet and white blaze down his face. Like his money making papa. He was leggy, bright eyed, and smart. And when he and his pals raced around the field he wouldn't let the other colts pass him. On a track he'll be a money maker.

While that was going on...

... in Saskatchewan

This colt is strong, powerful and big. His attitude ranges from surliness to "I dare ya!" Pretty flashy, too. Legs like pillars, feet like skillets and he has a power leap just this side of spectacular. He's bred to be a star. Nobody'll ride this one. He's bred for it.

5 horses. From 5 different parts of the country. Different in every way possible. But with all this in common, they were hard to break, harder to train and virtually impossible to stay on when they didn't want to be ridden. In fact, they could be dangerous.

Which makes each of them absolutely ideal for rodeos.

"Rock 'im with a big jump right outta the chute!"

"Classic run 'n' high kick. Let 'im think I'm easy."

"A fast stop 'n' lift to break 'im loose!"

"He's a goner! Calls for the victory lap!"

Saddle Broncs are true athletes; true competitors.
They'll do anything physically possible to unload the
rider. They compete with a whatever-it-takes attitude
and extraordinary athleticism and physicality.

When cowboys needed horses to do their job,
wild horses were rounded up and brought to
the ranch. It became the cowboy's job to get
a horse to accept a rider. Some were so good
at "bronc busting" they became pro's that
traveled from ranch to ranch.

All horses are born with buck in them. Some buck just to shake out the kinks every morning. Some buck when they're startled (the rustle of leaves will do it). The ones seen at a rodeo are the ones that simply don't want to be ridden.

"This won't take long."

"Kick real high; all 4 legs off the ground."

"He's comin' off. A good hip bump will loosen 'im up."

"Adios cowboy!"

Saddle broncs that are bred to buck probably have a touch of draft horse in their blood. That touch gives the horse the extra strength, power and durability that makes them ideal for long rodeo careers.

A simple move looks easy. But every move the bronc makes is a move made with incredible power that creates rider-misery. It's why the saddle is sometimes called the "hurricane deck!"

The way up may be soft, but the cowboy will tell
you that landing stiff legged on all fours is like
sitting on a pile driver.

"Two hops and she's hanging on for dear life!"

"Head down and solid high rear kick..."

"...and off she goes."

"Yahoo! I still got it."

The cowboy shifts a tiny bit forward. The bronc feels it and responds with a big head-down-rump-bump. The result is a cowboy hoping for a soft place to land.

More often than not, all it takes is a simple
move or two and the cowboy's looking to
land on all fours.

Talk about a snootful. Rider and horse are both diving. The bronc will handle it better. There's hardly anything a Saddle Bronc won't do to shuck the rider.

Just out of the chute. A classic move
in a classic battle. Ride'im cowboy!

The bronc's body is fully extended, neck stretched and head tilted slightly. Forelegs planted hard. The real high kick and quick twist to the right makes this bronc one tough ride.

The chute gate swings open. The bronc takes
a half-step and turns back into the chute and
tries to stand on his hind legs. A dangerous
situation for horse and rider.

In this case the pick-up rider isn't needed.
The cowboy is getting off with just a bit of
assistance from the bronc.

"Yahoo!"

A word about the life of a bucking horse...

Despite what you may hear or read, the bucking horses you see in a rodeo (local, state or national) are not brutalized or mistreated. Further, the controversial "Flank Strap" does not hurt or injure the horses. Remember, these horses are top professional athletes. They're treated quite well to help ensure a long and healthy rodeo career.

Flank Straps are not brutal. They may bother a horse, they may irritate the horse, they may even tickle some horses. Actually, the horse comes to associate the strap with performing; the horse works a bit harder to unload the rider. It's not unlike the crop or bat used by a jockey in a horse race. Flank Straps are thoughtfully and carefully made. The materials used are picked because they won't chafe, cut or abrade the horse. That's the short form.

Today about 30% of rodeo horses come from all sort of places, from all sorts of equine sports. The rest are a bred to buck. Regardless of where they come from, horses with exceptional bucking ability are usually sold to rodeo livestock contractors for fancy prices. Put simply, each horse represents an investment of some size. The contractors want their horses to really challenge the cowboys and keep spectators cheering. They can't do that if they're mistreated, hungry, or generally unwell. As the broncs mature, they're gentled and tamed in order to accept vaccinations, equine dentistry,worming etc. They're also taught how to load safely into trailers, to go into and come out of bucking chutes. Along with those measures the broncs are initially introduced to bucking work with cloth dummies in the saddle. Perhaps even more important, they're trained how to handle the intense eight seconds in which they and a rider battle it out... just for the helluvit!

Saddle bronc (riding) is the quintessential rodeo sport - not the chaos of bull riding or the thrashing of bareback riding. It might be harder than both.

~ John Branch
  Pulitzer Prize winner
  NY Times Sports Reporter

About David Ullman

"I have a camera with me just about everywhere I go. When I see something that catches my eye, something whimsical, interesting, evocative or exciting, I try to capture it. "It" being what my mind's eye sees. If I miss it, well, there's always another corner to turn."

"I was in the creative side of the advertising business for a long time. I worked with all kinds of photographers; learned a lot. While each approached their art from a different point of view, they all told me the same simple truth: "Every frame, good or bad, is a great lesson."

"I've spent a lot of time around horses. I competed on Hunters and Jumpers. They are athletic, graceful and quick. But the sheer power and ultra-athleticism of the Saddle Bronc is something else! And I tip my hat to the cowboys, It's a hard way to win a buckle."